TELLS

From The

LORD!

Tells From The Lord

Copyright © 2023 C. Campbell

All rights reserved.

ISBN:979-8-9878989-2-5

DEDICATION

This book is dedicated to our Lord and Savior. For bringing me back to a childhood dream that I had forgotten about and never thought of much anymore once my life started lifing. Through it all You Father have always been faithful, in spite of me. To each of you who reads this book. If He did it for me, He can do the same for you. There is nothing too hard for our God. No matter how you feel, what you have done, or what you have been through. Lord says in, **Jeremiah 1:5 (KJV)** Before I formed thee in the belly I knew thee; and before thou camest forth out of the womb I sanctified thee, and I ordained thee a prophet unto the nations.

Tells From The Lord

CONTENTS

Chapters

1	Your Mind….	1
2	Know Your Place….	Pg 11
3	Father's Absence….	Pg 21
4	Speak Only What Was Spoken….	Pg 28

Tells From The Lord

INTRODUCTION

Over these past few years, the Lord has been waking me up with phrases or a word, as I slept. When I hear Him, I'd get up and write down what He was saying. Once awaken, I would look the words up or go to the Bible and find scriptures related to His word and what He was telling me. Sometimes the words or phrase would be so powerful that I could not return to sleep, I could do nothing but fall on my knees and worship Him. Then there were times I did not understand what He was telling me. No matter what, I made sure I wrote it down as I heard it.

Now I would like to share with you some of these, **"Tells from the Lord."**

Tells From The Lord

CHAPTER 1

YOUR MIND

In this world today, you can see and hear all around, how the devil is destroying minds and coming against our thoughts. God woke me up one night to warn me, you, us, we. That the devil is coming after our mind. The devil is using depression, fear, shame, anxiety, hate, insecurity, rejection, lowliness, bitterness, self-righteousness, vanity, misunderstanding, assumptions, suicidal thoughts, violent actions and behavior, mental destruction, hurt, church hurt, condemnation, poverty, lack, feelings of worthlessness, and unforgiveness. Please hear me! The devil wants your mind, he uses sex, drugs, drinking, shame, anger, low self-esteem, isolation, hurt, trauma, molestation, and fear, to control our emotions and feelings. If he keeps us focusing on our problems, pain, and hurt, we will not think about, nor see the goodness of God, nor hear Him when He speaks.

The devil is using all types of distractions that seems normal or harmless. **Song of Solomon 2:15 (KJV)...the little foxes that spoil the vines....**
It is the little things, the little thoughts, the little pettiness, the little lies, the little deceit, that are not of God, we allow in our lives. That is what gives the devil room to operate. He makes us believe that these small things we think and do are harmless, funny, or popular (everyone else is doing it.). Like watching fight videos, crime channels, murder, horror, demon possession, witchcraft movies or shows. Those reality shows where they are always fighting and fussing with one another. Porn and sexual content movies and shows as well. Some of the places we go, certain music we listen to affects us too. As believers we must guard our hearts and mind. **Proverbs 4:23-27 (KJV) 23) Keep thy *heart* with all diligence; for out of it are the issues of life. 24) Put away from thee a forward *mouth*, and perverse lips put far from thee. 25) Let thine *eyes* look right on and let thine eyelids look straight before thee. 26) Ponder the path of thy *feet* and let all thy ways be established. 27) Turn not to the right hand nor to the left: remove thy foot from evil.**

The Bible is telling us to keep our heart, put away perverse lips, watch what we look at and where we go. The devil's trick is to have us thinking, we are in control. The trick is to keep us in bondage. If we are honest with ourselves, no matter what we indulge in, for how long, or how much, it only satisfies us for a moment. Have you ever thought that once you got this or achieved that, you would be happy and satisfied but once you get it, and achieved it, you were not as satisfied as you thought you would be? God is our source. He is our plug, and once you are plugged into Him, I confess there is no greater peace, joy, and satisfaction. We were created to serve Him and without Him our inner being(soul) has this void that we try to fill with things, people, and places, yet still feeling empty.

I remember watching a movie years ago. The character acted as if he was helpless and handicap. As he was telling these different stories and scenarios of this notorious bad guy; aka the "Devil" to the detectives. He makes this statement and it registered within me and I have not been able to forget it, because those words are true. At the end of the movie as the detectives are convinced that this guys, this handicap guy, was not a threat, a nobody. He is released and as he leaves out and is walking down the street, he starts to stand taller, his crooked and handicap body begins to straighten, and he now is walking normal. The quote, he quoted is by Charles Baudelaire; **'The greatest trick the Devil ever pulled was convincing the world he didn't exist.'** He was that bad guy, that aka "Devil." By him acting harmless and defenseless, he fooled the authorities and was set free.

The devil has many schemes and tricks. We must understand he has been at this for thousands of years. The bible says, in **1 Peter 5:8 (KJV) Be sober, be vigilant; because your adversary the devil, as a roaring lion, walketh about, seeking whom he may devour.** His trick is to have some of us to hate being alone, we surround ourselves with people and things, trying to fill a void only God can fill. God created us all for a purpose and the Devil knows it. **1 Peter 2:9 (KJV) But ye are a chosen generation, a royal priesthood, a holy nation, a peculiar people; that ye should shew forth the praises of Him who hath called you out of darkness into His marvelous light:**

For us that don't fit in, some may call themselves rejects. You don't understand why, but you do know it is something different in you. Even without giving things a lot of effort you still outshine them all. You even try and dumb yourself down to fit in. So, others want feel some type of way about you. It's not you, but the gift, the anointing, calling on your life. You need to take the time to connect with the Father.

I remember when I was in the world, trying to fit in, doing everything as the world but never being truly accepted and I would say, to myself; "I don't even fit in out here, where do I belong?" My brothers and sister's that is why you feel so alone and like an outcast, it is because God created you for so much more, than where you are, and what you see. We are a chosen generation, and the Devil wants to keep us feeling down, rejected, depressed, inadequate, and worthless. So, you will not realize the purpose and calling God has place on our life.

There are some of us (Christians), that think we are better than others (the self-righteous), but in reality, we are no better, than the next person. As I was reading in **Mark chapter 2 through chapter 3:1-6**. In these chapters it talks about how the Scribes and the Pharisees always had something to say about how Jesus conducted himself. In **Mark chapter 2: 1-6,** they had something to say about Him forgiving sin. In **Mark chapter 2: 13-17** they had a problem with Jesus sitting and eating with tax collectors and sinners. **Mark chapter 2: 18-22**, they had questions why His disciples did not fast. **Mark chapter 2:23-27** they had a problem with the disciples plunking the heads of grain on the Sabbath and eating. **Mark chapter 3:1-6** they had a problem with Jesus healing the man with the withered hand on the Sabbath. After reading this I was thinking, for them to see all these things, I wondered was they following Jesus or was it that many of them? The Scribes and Pharisees were religious leaders, priest, followers of the Law of Moses. They studied God's word, they read the prophecy yet, they could not see who Jesus was behind all their word and religion. I began to ask," why? For them as believers, religious rulers, and high priest, why did they have such a problem with what Jesus was doing and teaching?" The Lord said to me, 'There are "godly people" that don't believe in God! He said, "They just put on!"

This brought back to me when I worked at a restaurant as a line server, I had to work most Sundays. After church, I would rush to get home, get dress, and head off to work. I was on the usher board, I worked in the children's ministry once a month, and was on the soul winning team, that went out twice a month to witness. I was so amazed how the church folks treated me and the other servers on the line. Some of them were so, so rude, and talked to us as if we were beneath them and it took a lot for me to hold my tongue. I would hear the other servers say, 'That is why they don't go to church.' As a servant of God, I understood, their point of view, because in the world eyes, "If that's God, I'll pass." **1 John 4:20(KJV) If a man says, I love God, and hateth his brother, he is a liar:** Enough said! As representatives of Christ Jesus, we must let our light shine in darkness, because you don't know who is watching you. Your light should be on the hilltop, not hidden under a basket.

What, I am saying is nobody, none of us, is better than another. It is not our position, our pedigree, how much Bible we know, or what brands we wear, what we drive, where we live, or how well we speak. It does not matter how many scriptures we can quote, to be honest even the Devil knows the Word. We are all part of the body of Christ. **Romans 12:4(KJV) For as we have many members in one body, and all members have not the same office.** Everyone cannot be the face, eyes, mouth, head, or ears of the body. Somebody must be the toenail, elbow, or even the sole of the foot or armpit. You may not get the recognition you like the other parts, but the body, needs you to be whole. I don't care what part of the body I am, as long as I am connected to the Father. Don't allow the Devil to manipulate and distract you from your calling.

I know and understand that everyone that are suffering from any type of mental illness is Not, of the Devil. But there are many of us being tormented in our thoughts and mind. You try to hide it behind your looks, your education, your money, and laughter. Everybody comes to you, they like you, you are fun. They want to be with you and that is the problem. They come for the good time, for your looks, for what you can do for them, your figure (be it money or body) but they never stay for; "You!" The real, "You", not who you pretend to be. The hurting you, the messed up thinking you, the angry you, and the suffering in silence, you. God sees, "You", just as you are. He loves you enough, not to leave you there. You don't have to be perfect, you don't have to put on, and pretend for Him. He loves you. Right where you are, and He knows your name.

In the Bible, David's father did not consider calling him home, when God sent Samuel to his house to anoint a king. In **1 Samuel 16:10 (KJV) Again, Jesse made seven of his sons pass before Samuel. And Samuel said unto Jesse, The Lord hath not chosen these. 11. And Samuel said unto Jesse, Are here all thy children? And he said, there remaineth yet the youngest, and behold, he keepeth the sheep. And Samuel said unto Jesse, send and fetch him: for we will not sit down till he come hither.** Just as David, you may not have been invited in with the others but remember **1 Samuel 16:11 (KJV)** they could not sit down until he came.

We must understand the Devil. He hunts and torments your thoughts like that because he knows the plan God has for you and the calling on your life (**1 Peter 5:8 (KJV) Be sober, be vigilant; because your adversary (opponent) the devil, as a roaring lion, walketh about, seeking whom he may devour (destroy, prey, consume)** and if he can drown out your connection to God with self-righteous thinking, vanity, shame, worthlessness, anger, fear, depression, schizophrenia, anxiety. He can hold you back from the goodness of God. We have all heard the phrase; "Misery loves company," So think about it, the Devil once lived in the heavens, and woke it up each morning with songs and praises, until he wanted to take God's place and was casted down out of heaven. **Isaiah 14:12-14 (NKJV) How you are fallen from heaven, O Lucifer, son of the morning! How you are cut down to the ground, you who weakened the nations! 13. For you have said in your heart: I will ascend into heaven; I will exalt my throne above the stars of God; I will also sit on the mount of the congregation. On the farthest sides of the north; 14. I will ascend above the heights of the clouds; I will be like the Most High.**

The Devil does not want you to make heaven your home, because he was kicked out it. He became prideful and selfish. If you read the scriptures, you will read there are five **"I will"**, it was all about him. Now that he has been casted down, he does not want us, God's selected, God's chosen to make it in, either. That's why he fights you so hard, so strong and so much, to temp and distract you. God did not send Jesus into the world to die for Satan, but for you/us.

The Devil started working on me at a young age. Exposing me to perversion and even put the thought of suicide in my head, as a kid. I remember when I was running from getting a whipping, I had run down to the river where my dad, use to take us fishing and I heard a voice say, "Jump!" but as soon as I heard it, I said to myself, "I can't swim." I did not know it then, but it was the Devil wanting me to kill myself at the age of 7 or 8 years old (read more in Memories of a Broken Heart...but God). As I got older, I had a lot of challenges. I believed I was nothing and that I was worthless, because of the words that were spoken over me. I thought about killing myself, a lot. I was so insecure and broken.

I battled with depression, I was diagnosed with PTSD, and schizophrenia. The voices were so strong at times, I could not sleep. I played it off well, until I couldn't and on those days, I went into isolation. Taking the phone off the hook or turning the ringer off. I would not come to the door if anyone came over, no matter who it was. I stayed in the bed. I tried to keep it together for my kids. There were so many days that I wanted to die. I never thought I would live pass my 30's (read more in Memories of a Broken Heart...But God). I thank God I had enough in me to pray and to cry out to the Father and ask for help. We have lost so many people in this world, that were not able to fight those thoughts, or voices that plagued their mind. If you are dealing with similar issues, seek help, you are not alone. Email me and I will pray with and for you (sadreamerink.71@yahoo.com) I am not saying it is an easy journey, but you can overcome with the Lord's help. Even after I had given my life to Christ, the voices got stronger. As Joyce Meyers says, 'It is a battlefield in your mind."

There were times the voices were so loud and telling me I was nothing, and I was not worth the flesh I was in. I heard laughter, and taunting saying, how I am not good enough for God. I remember one day just crying and pleading with the Father and asking Him to help me! Please stop the noise in my head. The Lord reminded me, how Jesus used the scriptures when the Devil came to temp Him after He had fasted 40 days and forty nights. **Matthew 4:1-11(KJV)** If you read those scriptures, you will read how each time the devil said anything, Jesus would say, 'It is written" and throw the Word back at the Devil. Then finally saying, in verse **10; 'Get the hence, Satan: for it is written, thou shalt worship the Lord thy God, and Him only shalt thou serve. 11. Then the devil leaveth Him, and behold angels came and ministered unto Him.**

I now do what the scriptures says Jesus did. I now speak and throw the Word back at the Devil when he attacks my thoughts. I take back control and let the devil know, I don't belong to him.

Philippians 4:8 (KJV) Finally, brethren, whatsoever things are true, whatsoever things are honest, whatsoever things are just, whatsoever things are pure, whatsoever things are lovely, whatsoever things are of good report; if there be any praise, think on these things.

1 John 4:4 (KJV) "Ye are of God, little children, and have overcome them: greater is He that is in me than he that is in the world."

Psalm 118:17 "I shall not die, but live, and declare the works of the Lord."

Psalm 139: 14 (NKJV) "I will praise You, for I am fearfully and wonderfully made; Marvelous are Your works, and that my soul knows very well."

These are just a few of the scriptures I say back to the voices when they try to creep in. I let them know, "Not Today!" I take back control of my thoughts, in Jesus's name.

Disclaimer

Mental health is a serious thing. I am not saying everyone that is suffering from mental health issues is fighting a spirit or it is the devil. I am no doctor, nor mental health expert. I am just sharing my experience.

CHAPTER 2

KNOW YOUR PLACE

Everything under the sun has a place, a spot, an area where God placed it. You can read all about it in Genesis chapter 1. God placed everything in its rightful spot according to His purpose and plan. The sun, moon, stars, heaven, earth, clouds, morning, darkness, land, waters, trees, grass, and every living creature and God said, "It was good," male and female. Even then, in Genesis when God brought the woman to Adam, Adam knew their place. **Genesis 2:24 (NKJV) Therefore a man shall leave his father and mother and be joined to his wife, and they shall become one flesh.** How did Adam know that? Because he had no parents, God created him of the dust of the ground. **Genesis 2:7 (NKJV) And the Lord God formed man of the dust of the ground and breathed into his nostrils the breath of life; and man became a living being.** Yet, he knew their place (their purpose, their area).

1 Samuel 16, you can read the story of King David. You will read how David was in his rightful place, his spot, the area where he was supposed to be. When Samuel came to the house of Jesse to anoint one of his sons, king. Even though none of the sons of Jesse that were before Samuel was the one God wanted him to anoint. Samuel asked Jesse was there another? Jesse knew where his youngest son was. In the field attending to the sheep and when David was called to come, he was found in the area, in the place he was supposed to be. They did not have to look for him or send out a search party to go find him.

1 Samuel 16: 11,12 (KJV) 11. And Samuel said unto Jesse, Are here all thy children? And he said, 'There remaineth yet the youngest, and behold, he keepeth the sheep.' And Samuel said unto Jesse, send and fetch him: for we will not sit down till he come hither. 12. And he sent and brought him in. Now he was ruddy, and withal of a beautiful countenance, and goodly to look to. And the Lord said, Arise, anoint him: for this is he. The scripture says in **1 Samuel 16:13 (KJV) Then Samuel took the horn of oil and anointed him in the midst of his brethren: and the Spirit of the Lord came upon David from that day forward. So, Samuel rose, and went to Ramah.**

Even after Samuel had anointed David; David went back to attending to the sheep. See right there, David could have gotten the bighead and flaunted that he was anointed king. He could have bragged and boasted to his brothers about how he had been chosen over them, but he didn't, he went back to his place. **Verse 13** says that the Spirit of the Lord came upon David from that day forward. I can imagine while David was out in the field that the Lord was working on him, preparing him, ministering to him, building him, and strengthening him for the battles he was about to face, in his life. Soon after **1 Samuel 16:15-23** David was invited to play for the king when those evil spirits came upon him. David was loved by King Saul and became his armourbearer.

David had three brothers that fought in the army of King Saul. David's father told David to take his brother's and others some food and take the cheese to the captain. As David was talking to them **1 Samuel 17:23(KJV),** there came Goliath trash talking against the king and his God and he inquired what would be the reward of one who defeats this uncircumcised Philistine **1 Samuel 17:25-27(KJV).** His brother chastised him and tried to belittle him by asking why he was not tending to those few sheep. **1 Samuel 17:28 (KJV)**

David goes up against Goliath. Goliath cursed David and took him as a joke. David slew Goliath by the name of the Living God **1 Samuel 17:43-51** and cuts Goliath's head off with his own sword. King Saul was astonished and amazed at this young man and welcomed him in, but once King Saul heard the song, the women song of him killing thousands and David killing ten thousand, King Saul was jealous, and began to hate him. **1 Samuel 18:6,7**

David ran from King Saul in **1 Samuel chapter 18** till the death of King Saul in **Chapter 31. In the 24th chapter of 1 Samuel** David has an opportunity to kill the King. When David and his men were hiding in the cave and King Saul came in. David's men told him God had delivered King Saul into his hand to kill him and David cut off a piece of King Saul's robe. After doing that David's heart was grieved because David respected the calling on King Saul's life even though the spirit of the Lord had left Saul, David respected the king. **1 Samuel 16:14 (KJV)**. But he, would not allow himself or his men to hurt King Saul. David did let King Saul know that he could have taken his life. David said in **1 Samuel 24:12 (KJV) The Lord judge between me and thee and the Lord avenge me of thee but mine hand shall not be upon thee: 13. As saith the Proverd of the ancients, Wickedness proceedeth from the wicked: but my hand shall not be upon thee.**

With that being said, Saul wept (cried) and called David a righteous man (verse17). In **1 Samuel verse 19, 20** Saul told David the Lord would reward him and surely, he shall be king of Israel. In **chapter 26** King Saul still sought, to kill David. Once again David had an opportunity to kill the king, but the respect David had for the anointing on King Saul's life David would not allow himself, nor his men to kill the king, because David knew his place. **1 Samuel 26:5-25 (NKJV)** For David knew God put him in that place, he did not ask for it, he did not seek that position out. I am sure if he knew how that anointing was going affect his life, he might not have wanted it, but he knew God called him to it and when it was time, God was going to place him in it. Our God does not need our help, just our trust, obedience, and patience.

When God tells us or shows us bits and pieces of where He is going to take us, or what He is about to do in our life. We still must know our place and wait on God. While waiting, prepare your mind, and heart. Ask God to show you; you. And areas you need to work on. When I was in prison and God laid on my heart not to return to Athens, where I was born and raised. I did not understand, I started looking for transitional housing, that I could apply for and would allow me to live with my children, but I kept getting turned down.

I later asked my counselor at the prison about the "Work release center". About six months later I was told to pack up in the middle of the night and driven to Atlanta, Ga., to a women's work release center. After about four months, my counselor said the parole board needed an address ASAP because they were about to give me a release date. It had to be an address with a land line. I knew my mom house phone was off at the moment. I decided to call my sister and asked her husband if I could give their address and phone number. He turned me down, after first telling me yes, then after passing the phone to my sister he told her to tell me, "No!" It was like a punch in the gut. I could not understand it, because I knew I heard from God so why was I getting rejected?

When God placed **Genesis 12:1-4 (NKJV)** in my spirit, I said, "Lord if this is You; You do it!". Yet I tried to do it and find a place myself because I forgot my place. I thought I would help God out. I thought I would do the leg work because that's what us humans do, right (try to figure it out)? God had given me Genesis 12 (KJV) (read my testimony "Memories of a Broken Heart..But God") In chapter **12:1, the Lord had said unto Abram, Get out of thy country, and from thy kindred, and from thy father's house,** *unto a land that I will shew thee*: There it is, the Lord said, "unto a land that I will shew thee." I did not know my place and I tried to help God out. God did not need my help, just my trust, obedience, and patience.

After the rejection, after crying, after questioning God and second guessing what He had told me. I will say about a week later a young lady that I had seen in passing, started talking to me, out the blue. Telling me about an organization that helps inmates that are getting released. This organization helped me get a place. This lady never really talked to me, excepted a "Hi!" in crossing. There she gave me all the information and I went to my counselor and was given the greenlight to go and talk with them. This organization helped me to get an apartment. They paid my first month's rent, half of my second month's rent and a third of my third month's rent. They bought me $200 worth of groceries and $200 of new clothes and I was allowed to pick out $750 of brand-new furniture. I said that to say this, if the Lord has given you instructions or has laid anything on your heart, settle your spirit and know your place and you too will be saying, " God Did It! "

Trust me, whatever the Lord has laid on your heart, or in your spirit. Trust Him, even if you have just started on your journey of obedience. Trust Him to lead the way. As in **Proverbs 3:5,6 (NKJV) Trust in the Lord with all your heart and lean not on your own understanding; In all your ways acknowledge Him, and He shall direct your paths.**

There will be battles and attacks you did not expect. People turning on you that you never thought would. Situations happening that will have you, speechless. Just talk to the Lord and say, "I don't like it, but I trust You! Lord, it hurts, but I trust You! Lord, it does not feel good, but I trust You! Lord, I don't understand, but I trust You! Lord, I don't see a way out, but I trust You! Continue to lean and depend on Him and remember **1 Thessalonians 5:24 (NKJV) He who calls you is faithful, who also will do it.** He called you; He will cover you and keep you as long as you know your place and don't give up.

There are a lot of people in the Bible that knew their place. In **Daniel 3:8-29 (NKJV)** Shadrach, Meshach, and Abed-Nego. They refused to bow down and worship the king's golden image and was thrown into the furnace. Before they were thrown into the furnace, the king had the furnace heated up seven times hotter than it usually was and he asked them this question in **verse 15**. Who is the god who will deliver you from my hands? I love their answer in **Daniel 3: 16-18 (NKJV) 16...O Nebuchadnezzar we have no need to answer you this matter. 17. If that is the case, our God whom we serve is able to deliver us from the burning fiery furnace, and He will deliver us from your hand, O king. 18. But if not, let it be known to you, O King, that we do not serve your gods, nor will we worship the gold image which you have set up."**

They knew their place to the point they said, "But if not." Even if our God does not save us from this furnace, we still are not worshipping your golden image! PERIOD!!! To me that shows their level of trust, faith, love, respect, honor, and belief they had for their God. Powerful!

In **Daniel 6:1-28 (NKJV)** You will read (paraphrasing) about Daniel who was distinguished and had an excellent spirit. The king was considering putting Daniel over the whole realm, above the Satraps (provincial governor) and Governors. Them knowing the thoughts of the king, the Satraps and Governors sought to find some dirt against Daniel (there is always someone that wants what you have but can't handle what they got!). They could not find anything or any fault against Daniel concerning the kingdom, because he was faithful. So, they decided to come up with something concerning his God.

They went before the king with a royal statute to make a firm decree, that no one should petition (call upon, worship) any other god or man for thirty days except the king or they would be cast into the den of lions. The king agreed, and they drew up the decree in a way that it could not be changed, according to the law of the Medes and Persians which altered not. Daniel knew the decree was signed but he still went and prayed as he has always done three times a day in front of his window. His haters waited and watched so they could go tell on him. What they did not know was Daniel knew his place. No written decree was going to stop him from praying and giving thanks to his God.

They knew the king favored Daniel and when the king heard it was Daniel that was caught praying, the king was displeased with himself, and he thought of a way to save Daniel from his decree till the sun went down. But the haters gonna hate and they came to the king letting him know he had to do it and no take backs. So, the king gave the command, and they brought Daniel to cast him in the lion's den, but the king went to Daniel and said, "your God, whom you serve continually, He will deliver you **(Daniel 6:16 NKJV)**

The king is telling Daniel that his God would deliver him. By Daniel knowing his place made the people around him, know his place and his God, because the king knew greater was in Daniel, than he that is in the world. (**1 John 4:4 KJV**) After Daniel was cast in the lion's den, the king fasted, he could not even sleep **(Daniel 6:18 KJV)**.

The part that gets me is that the Satraps and Governors came up with that decree. Got the king to agree to it for 30 days. The king only was to be worshipped and praised, but because of Daniel the king was fasting and loss sleep praying and worshiping Daniel's God (he broke his own decree). **Daniel 6:19,20 (NKJV)** The first thing that morning the king aroused early and went to the den and called out to Daniel saying the servant of the Living God. Has your God whom you serve continually, deliver you? The king went from a man seeking praise, to a man giving praise to the only true living God of Daniel. Oh! Those haters, their children, and families took Daniel's place in the lion's den.

The Bible is also full of some that did not, know their place. **2 King** in **chapter 5 (NKJV)**(paraphrasing). There was this commander named Naaman in Syria. He was a great and honorable man before his master and a mighty man of valor, but he was a leper. After winning a battle they brought back some captives. One was a young lady from Israel that waited on Naaman's wife. She tells his wife that God is with the prophet in Samaria and could heal her husband. The king wrote a letter to the king of Israel requesting that his servant may be healed of his leprosy.

Long story short, **2 Kings 5:9-13 (NKJV)**(paraphrasing). Naaman got healed from his leprosy by obeying the instructions of the prophet Elisha. At first, he was in his feelings because the prophet did not meet with him face to face, when he showed up at his house but sent instructions out to him by his messenger telling him to go wash in the Jordan river seven times and his flesh shall be restored. Naaman, really got an attitude and became furious when he learned Elisha wanted him to go wash in the Jordan river. Naaman, had expectations of how he thought the man of God was going to restore him (heal his leprous), (this is not the point I am trying to make, but there is a story in this too). He eventually did what he was told by a little push from his maid servant and was healed.

After being healed he returned to Elisha, saying **in 2 kings 5:15(NKJV) ...Indeed, now I know that there is no God in all the earth, except in Israel...** He had brought Elisha all types of gifts. In verse **16(NKJV) Elisha says, "As the Lord lives, before whom I stand, I will receive nothing. Naaman urged him to take it, but Elisha refused. Verse 19, Elisha tells him to go in peace.**

2 King 5:20-27 (NKJV)(paraphrasing) Then comes Gehazi, Elisha's servant and I am sure he was listening to Naaman and Elisha's conversation and saw the many gifts Naaman wanted to give Elisha and immediately Gehazi forgot his place. He thought about what Elisha had done for Naaman and these things Naaman wanted to give Elisha and greed took over. He ran after Naaman and when he stopped, he told Naaman that Elisha sent him saying, give a talent of silver and two changes of garments.

Naaman was happy to give it not knowing it was a lie. He even gave him an extra talent. After receiving the items Gehazi stored them away in the house. Later he went and stood before Elisha. Elisha asked him where he went and Gehazi lied and said he did not go anywhere (Gehazi forgot his place). By doing all of that and lying, Elisha told him that the leprosy of Naaman, shall now cling to him and his descendants (his children) forever and Gehazi left out as white as snow.

Tell me was there ever a time when you forgot your place? I would love to hear about it. (sadreamerink.71@yahoo.com)

CHAPTER 3

THE FATHER'S ABSENCE

*Absence-the state of being away from a place person

*Absence-Nonexistence or lack of

When God spoke this phase to me, I really did not know which way I was supposed to go with it. Did we really need another book on "Absence Fathers", and how their absence affects the family as a unit and a child's development? Whether if the father is out of the home or in it, but distance. I struggled within, with my own daddy issues, and to be honest I did not know what the Lord wanted me to talk about. That had not been said before, by many others. So, I began jotting down everything that came to me. When God dropped "The Father's Absence" in my spirit, I had no clue or ideal at the time I would be writing this book. I just knew the Lord was telling me something.

Once I knew all the words and phrases were for a book, I really had to go before my Father God and ask the Holy Spirit for guidance on what He wanted me to say. I began to write but got nothing. I finished a paragraph and nothing. I would step away for days, hoping the Holy Spirit would speak to me, but nothing. I began to pray and ask God what it was, He wanted me to say. I even considered removing this topic, but I knew belonged. So, I continued to pray and ask for guidance.

Weeks had passed and one day while sitting in front of my computer, praying, and asking God for direction, before heading off to work. I asked God again, "What is it that I am supposed to talk about?" Then I heard, **"I'm the Father and they are operating in absence of Me!"** When I heard that, it blew my mind, it registered in with my spirit instantly. Today there are so many leaders preaching, teaching, leading, in the Father's absence.

A lot of us as 'Christians' are not following the Word of God. We are only following the part of the Word, we like, or that comes easy to us. There is more to this Christian walk than confessing and believing God raised Jesus from the dead. We are to be Christ like! Years ago, in my earlier walk with the Lord, I did not fully understand what having a relationship with the Father, really meant. I had not yet learned or knew how to totally depend and lean on the Him. I had real trust issues, of any and everyone, because of my past experiences. I chalked it up as not being a people's person or not liking people and I did not mind sharing my feeling or belief. The funny thing about that is once I shared my feelings on how I felt, others who felt the same way, came and shared their feelings with me.

As I grew more in my knowledge of God and His Word, the question came to me, "How could I call myself a Christian and not like people?" I thought I was justified because of all the things I went through dealing with people. The Word says in, **1 John 4:20 (NKJV) Of anyone says, "I love God." And hates his brother is a liar; for he that does not love his brother whom he has seen, how can he love God whom he has not seen?**

God let me know it was in the Father's absence, I had people issues. I allowed people access to my life. You may ask, "What do I mean?" I picked friends who were interesting to me. I allowed people to come in my life and I did not notice or see what their true intentions were, because I was so caught up in having a good time, on their looks, their money, the conversations, and, or out of loneliness. I did not have a true relationship with God, and I did not allow Him to direct me (What? You need God to direct you in relationships and friendships? YES!). There were times when I met certain people and it would be something about them that was unsettling, and I would distance myself from them. Then there were some who I really liked, and they ghosted me as fast as we met. I was devastated by their action, but what I did not understand then, and saw later, that I was saved by that ghosted action and that unsettling within, helped me dodged that bullet.

In those days, I did not have that connection with the Father I have today. I now understand God sees farther than any of us can. He knows the end before the beginning. **Isaiah 46:10 (NKJV) Declaring the end from the beginning, and from ancient times the things that are not yet done, saying, My counsel shall stand, and I will do all my pleasure: Isaiah 46:10 (NIV), '**

Now, I am learning we must be intentional of who we allow access to our life. Everyone is not a friend, and some are only there to profit off you, to hinder, and hold you back from the will and plan of God. They see the potential and purpose you have on your life even if you don't. Think about how, Jesus, healed, delivered, and cast out unclean spirits. Many wanted to be with Him, yet out of all those people, He only allowed a selected 12, to be in His circle. It was fewer than that on certain occasions **(Mark 5: 36,37 (NKJV)** the young girl Jesus restored to life) **(Mark 9:1-3 (NKJV)** when Jesus transfigured before them and appeared Elijah and Moses)

You may say, "Judas betrayed Jesus." Yes, Jesus allowed Judas in His circle because Judas had a part to play in His crucifixion, in His death, for His resurrection. After Judas played his part, then he killed himself. **(Matthew 27:3-5 NKJV) 3. Then Judas, His betrayer, seeing that He had been condemned, was remorseful and brought back the thirty pieces of silver to the chief priest and elders, 4. saying "I have sinned by betraying innocent blood." And they said, "What is that to us? You see to it!" 5. Then he threw down the pieces of silver in the temple and departed and went and hanged himself.**
Please hear me and hear me well. No man took Jesus's life, He and the Father in heaven set that up, to save us! **John 10:18 (KJV)** Jesus says, **"No man taketh it from me, but I lay it down of myself. I have power to lay it down, and I have power to take it again. This commandment have I received of my Father."** I make known the end from the beginning, from ancient times, what is still to come. I say, 'My purpose will stand, and I will do all that I please.'

I remember years ago; I was watching a well-known pastor preach and he started talking about the Father's (God) love. He gave an example of how his daughter came to him and asked for some money. He shared she asked, and he said yes, but instead of her going to get the money out of his room, she walks towards the door. He tells her to wait, the money is in the other room. She replies, "I knew you would say yes, so I already got it." He goes on to say, that is how God wants us to approach Him with boldness and confidence that He will, with pleasure grant our request

Unlike his daughter, I never had the experience of going to my earthly father, asking and he freely gave. I did not know how that felt. That made me realize that's why I had such a lack of trust and faith in my heavenly Father, because I was comparing Him to my earthly father. In the book of **Hebrews 11:6 (KJV) But without faith it is impossible to please Him: for he that cometh to God must believe that He is, and that He is a rewarder of them that diligently seek Him.** I realize I did not genuinely believe in God. Going to church did not make me a believer. Working in the church did not increase my faith. I treated God (the Father) as a man. When the issues of life began to happen, I prayed less and tried to handle it the best way I could and I ended up defeated, depressed, broken, and blaming God. But it was the absence(lack) of the Father in my life, that hindered my trust and faith. My relationship with the Father was not strong enough because, I was not praying (only when I needed something), nor did I spend time with Him (in the Word), I lacked the confidence in knowing He is faithful.

I was very independent, and I learned I could not be independent and truly trust God, because He says in **Isaiah 55:8,9 (NKJV) 'For My thoughts are not your thoughts, nor are your ways My ways,' says the Lord. 9. For as the heavens are higher than the earth, So, are My ways higher than your ways, and My thoughts than your thoughts.**

When I wanted or needed things done, I stepped ahead of God and did them, but it always cost me more, than if I would have just waited on Him. I have messed up so much operating in the Father's absence and in my own strength. Not going to Him in prayer, not asking for His guidance, not trusting in Him enough to understand how much He truly loved and cared for my well-being.

As I continued growing in my walk with God; God continued to deal with me, and show me, me. He brought my attention back to the story about of the children of Israel in the book of Exodus, Leviticus, Numbers, etc. God reminded me of something I said when I first started reading about them and how they complained after all the miracles God had performed before them. Back then as I was reading about the children of Israel, I was judgmental and thought how ungrateful they were. In actuality, I was doing the same thing. Complaining, doubting, not trusting, not believing, and forgetting about all the things He had already done in my life. Things I had bragged to others about at first but soon forgot. That hit me hard and made me realize, there was some Israel in me. That is why it took me a while to reach this position I am in today, because of the complaining, the doubting, unbelief, and the lack of confidence in Him and myself. I realize I only trust God in what I thought was possible. Never really looking at the ability that He is God, and that there is nothing too hard or too big for Him.

I learned, if we really are desiring a change, a new outcome, a new perspective on, and in life. We have to stop operating in our Father's absence. Open your bible and spend more time in the Word, build a relationship with Him personally. Get to know the Father for yourself. Apply His Word to your life. The same way you built that relationship with your husband, wife, friends, co-workers, and staff. Take time and build a relationship with the Father, spend time with Him, seek His face, and be obedient to His will and word. Keep His commandments and watch Him change your life. Every day is not going to be sunshine, and roses just remember He is your strength in your time of weakness, He will never leave you alone, nor forsake you. Even in the days you stumble and fall get back up, repent, forgive yourself, and know you are still a child of God, even on your worst days. He loves with an everlasting love. **Proverbs 24:16 (KJV) For a just man falleth seven times, and riseth up again: but the wicked shall fall into mischief.**

To the leaders and overseers of God's sheep. Thus says the Lord, so take heed. There are too many churches today operating in the Father's absence and working in their own agenda. The Lord told me, "You see what is happening now, since prayer was taken out of schools. Stop taking Me out the church and operating in My (The Father's) absence!

Chapter 4

SPEAK ONLY WHAT WAS SPOKEN

There is an "Importance" in this chapter's statement as a child of God. To the degree that it is mentioned twice in the Bible.

Deuteronomy 4:2(NKJV) "You shall not add to the word which I command you, nor take from it, that you may keep the commandments of the Lord your God which I command you."

Revelation 22:18-19(NKJV) "For I testify to everyone who hears the words of the prophecy of this book: If anyone adds to these things, God will add to him the plaques that are written in this book: and if anyone takes away from the words of the book of this prophecy, God shall take away his part from the Book of Life, from the holy city, and from the things which are written in this book."

Tells From The Lord

This is just a reminder, to anyone the Lord has given a word to speak. Say only what was spoken. If you are new to the Lord giving you a word to say. There is a moment of unease to some because we don't know how it will be received. I remember my first time having a nudge in my spirit to say and give someone something. I failed miserably.

At the time I had just gotten out of prison and was in a new city, a new apartment, starting a new walk with Christ. I did not know anyone in the area, accept a lady from the prison that stayed in the same apartments complex. We never saw each other much. I had bought some "Chick" gospel tracts and would leave one in each seat on each bus I got off. One day while waiting for the bus a lady walked up. While we were both standing at that bus stop, I heard the Holy Spirit say give her a tract, and tell her, "Everything will be alright." After hearing those words, I could not move. My stomach felt like it had knots in it, and I could not move. Fear overcame me like a blanket, and I could not speak or move, I was like that for ten minutes before the bus came.

After getting on the bus, I felt so bad and ashamed. I did not understand what that feeling was, then because right after my thoughts began to torment me and letting me know how unworthy I truly was and that lead to a pity party (the devil is so calculating and deceiving), a couple months later I visited a church across the street from where I lived and started going regularly. I liked how they preached on supporting one another in the church in business. It was a guy in there that sold meats. I am working and I thought that maybe I could start selling wing plates like I did in Athens on the side to make extra money.

I get the guy's number from the church that sold meat and I call him to ask about his wing prices. I asked him how much a case of wings was. When a say case I mean a 40lb box of wings. He told me $120; he also said it would be (6) 10lb bags. I thought that was a little expensive, but I chalked it up to I had been locked up 33 months and was now I am living in a new area. I agreed on the sale and gave him my address because he delivered. The whole time while waiting on him, the Holy Spirit tells me not to do it. The Holy Spirit told me to call him and cancel the order, "Don't Do It!" but I felt I would be perceived and looked at some type of way by the member of the church for not keeping the agreement.

The guy comes and bring that big box into the house, and I pay him not looking at what he brought. He leaves, I drag the box to the sink where I have my gloves and zip lock bags ready to wash and separate. When I open the box, I was devasted. It was 6 bags of store-bought chicken wings on ice. These were bags you buy at the grocery store for $6.99 (at the time 2004) a bag. I could not believe this man, this Christian, got over on me like that, but the Holy Spirit did warn me, but I was so concern about how it would look on me for canceling, that ended up paying almost 3 times more than it was worth.

Moments like those taught me the important of being obedient. That sad feeling within was the Holy Spirit grieving, at my disobedient. **Ephesians 4:30(NKJV) And do not grieve the Holy Spirit of God, by whom you were sealed for the day of redemption.**

This leads me to the next, tell from the Lord: It amazes me how the Lord works. One night as I was up reading, and Lord starts speaking and I started writing.**1 king 22:1(KJV)** Three years had passed with no war, conflict, or fighting, between Syria and Israel. Jehoshaphat king of Judea comes to visit Ahab, the king of Israel. **1 King 16:29-33(NKJV)** Ahab the son of Omri became king to reign over Israel. He reigned over Israel in Samaria 22 years and did more to provoke the Lord God of Israel, more than all who were before him. On top of that he took a wife (Jezebel) the daughter of Ethbaal, king of the Sidonians, and he went and served Baal. He also reared up an altar and made a grove for Baal in the house of Baal, which he built in Samaria.

1 King 22: 3-6 (NKJV) Shortly after arriving Ahab starts to tell Jehoshaphat how Ramoth in Gilead is theirs and how they had failed to retrieve it from the king of Syria. Ahab wants to know will the king of Judea would accompany him in battle, to take back their land. The king of Judea agrees to join him and let Ahab know, his people, is his people, and his horses are his horses. But King Jehoshaphat asked if Ahab would inquire for the word of the Lord, first.

The king of Israel gathered 400 of his prophets and asked them if they should go against Ramoth in Gilead to fight or refrain? All the prophets said, "GO." the Lord shall deliver it into your hand, but for some reason King Jehoshaphat was not satisfied, and asked, "Was there another prophet of the Lord here, that they could ask?" I believe King Jehoshaphat knew just because everybody is saying it, does not always make it true.

This part of the story brought me back to a time before accepting Christ into my life when I partied. Some of the people I had visited were going to a club, I had not planned on going out that night, plus I had my son with me, and I did not have money for that, yet everyone was telling me to come, encouraging me to go out with them. The crazy part was I knew none of them really liked me and had done and said things against me in the past. An old friend of mines also agreed to pay my way in and buy the drinks. I had not been out in a while, and everyone was cheering me on. I decided to go. I walk my son up to his grandmother's house and before I left, my son that night he looked at me and said, "Mama don't go." I went anyway and that night changed my life.

1 King 22:8-12(NKJV) Ahab knew of another prophet, but he hated him because he never prophesies anything good concerning him. Nevertheless, Ahab sent his officer to bring the prophet Micaiah, son of Imlah, quickly. While they waited for Micaiah, the kings each put on their robes and sat each on his throne, at a threshing floor at the entrance of Samaria, while all the other prophets, prophesied before them. One of his prophets named Zedekiah made them horns of iron and said, "Thus said the Lord, 'With these you shall gore the Syrians until they are destroyed.' As the other prophets encouraged them to go and said, that the Lord would deliver the land to them.

When the officer comes to Micaiah, he lets him know the other prophets are all on one accord and are encouraging the king. He even says, "let your word be like them, encouraging. But Micaiah, says, "As the Lord lives, whatever the Lord says to me, that will I speak."

After arriving the king asked Micaiah, "Shall we go to war against Ramoth Gilead, or shall we refrain?" I guess Micaiah tries to comply and tell the king what he wants to hear, because he says in verse 15. Go and prosper, for the Lord will deliver it into the hand of the king. I don't know how king Ahab knew what he was saying was not the truth. Maybe Micaiah had a little smirk on his face or something. Whatever it was it made the king ask him again and this time Micaiah says, "I saw all Israel scattered on the mountains, as sheep that have no shepherd. And the Lord said, "These have no master. Let each return to his house in peace."

After hearing that King Ahab tells King Jehoshaphat, "Did I not tell you he would not prophesy good but evil concerning me?" It's funny to me, how we get upset at the truth, even when we are the ones searching for it? Micaiah did not come to them with answer, the king sent for him.

Verse 19-23 Micaiah goes on to tell them, "Therefore hear the word of the Lord: I saw the Lord sitting on His throne, and all the host of heaven standing by, on His right hand and on His left. The Lord said, "Who will persuade Ahab to go up, that he may fall at Ramoth Gilead?" One spoke in this manner, and another spoke in this manner. Then the spirit came forward and stood before the Lord and said, I will persuade him." The Lord said to him, 'In what why?' I will go out and be a lying spirit in the mouth of all the prophets.' And the Lord said, "You shall persuade him and prevail. Go out and do so.'

Micaiah goes on to say, "The Lord has put a lying spirit of all these prophets of yours, and the Lord has declared disaster against you." Even with hearing the words of Micaiah, King Ahab dismissed it. That is how it is. The signs are there, the words of warning have been spoken. For some reason you feel as if you will be alright. I felt like that, that night. I had not been out in a while, first time at this new club, friends calling my name that I had not seen in months. I'm happy and feeling good and over there, over there, they were plotting against me, and I fell for it. I did not take heed of the words my 10 years old son spoke to me; "Mama don't go." But I thank the Lord; He did not take my life because hell would have been my home if He had allowed death to take me. I thank God for not giving us what we deserve.

Verse 24-28 Zedekiah, one of Ahab's prophets, struck Micaiah on the cheek and asked him, "which way did the spirit from the Lord go from me to speak to you?" And Micaiah said, "Indeed you shall see on that day, when you go into the inner chambers to hide!" Ahab had Micaiah taken to Amon the governor of the city to be put in prison and told them to feed him bread and water of affliction until he returns in peace. Micaiah said, "If you ever return in peace, the Lord has not spoken it to me." And he said, "Take heed, all you people!"

I know being the voice of the Lord is not always going to be received with opened arms and sometimes it's not popular to speak truth, even when they ask you for it, in church, with family and friends. Just remember to be obedient to the voice and word of God. Remember it's not all about having a word from God, but about speaking only what was spoken, and don't forget to speak it, in love.

I would like to thank you for taking time out and reading this book. If you would like to accept Jesus Christ as our Lord and Savior, the bible says in **Romans 10:9(KJV) That if you confess with your mouth the Lord Jesus, and shalt believe in thine heart that God hath raised Him from the dead, thou shalt be saved.** If you confess and believe in your heart, you my brother/sister are saved. Find you a bible teaching church and welcome to the family of Christ!

Tells From The Lord

Made in the USA
Coppell, TX
30 December 2023